EDGE BOOKS™

Not Your Ordinary Trivia

VIDEO GAME
TRIVIA

What You Never Knew About
Popular Games, Design Secrets
and the Coolest Characters

Raintree is an imprint of Capstone Global Library Limited, a company incorporated in England and Wales having its registered office at 264 Banbury Road, Oxford, OX2 7DY – Registered company number: 6695582

www.raintree.co.uk
myorders@raintree.co.uk

Edited by Mandy Robbins
Designed by Juliette Peters
Picture research by Jo Miller
Production by Tori Abraham
Originated by Capstone Global Library Ltd
Printed and bound in India

ISBN 978 1 4747 5943 4
22 21 20 19 18
10 9 8 7 6 5 4 3 2 1

British Library Cataloguing in Publication Data
A full catalogue record for this book is available from the British Library.

Acknowledgements
We would like to thank the following for permission to reproduce photographs: Alamy: Archive PL, 8b, Game Shots, 17, Marc Tielemans, 16, Pete Jenkins, 19 (inset), razorpix, 18, 20t; AP Images : Paul Sakuma, 11t; Getty Images: Sascha Steinbach/Stringer, 7; Newscom: imageBROKER/Jochen Tack, 12, KRT/MBR, 21t, REUTERS/Issei Kato, 13b, REUTERS/Jason Redmond, 15; Shutterstock: Africa Studio, 11b, alphaspirit, 4-5, Anna Chernova, cover (clouds), bestv, 6r, Bobnevv, 27, chrnsitr, 10, chuckchee, cover (game scene), CREATISTA, 22, Dan Thornberg, 8t, Dikiiy, 29, evgeny kondrashov, 24b, furtseff, 26b, hedgehog111, 6l, Jeramey Lende, 9t, Matthew Corley, 28t, OlegDoroshin, 14t, OleksandrO, 23b, ostill, 13t, Pavel L Photo and Video, 25, Pe3k, 9b, Refluo, 14b, rkl_foto, 26t, Roman Kosolapov, 23t, Shaun Robinson, 19t, Tinseltown, 20b, Untashable, 32, vipman, 19b, winui, 28b, xiaorui, 21b; U.S. Marine Corps photo by Cpl. Demetrius Morgan, 24t
Design elements: Shutterstock: Anna Chernova, chuckchee, Untashable

The publisher does not endorse products whose logos may appear on objects in images in this book.

Every effort has been made to contact copyright holders of material reproduced in this book. Any omissions will be rectified in subsequent printings if notice is given to the publisher.

All the Internet addresses (URLs) given in this book were valid at the time of going to press. However, due to the dynamic nature of the Internet, some addresses may have changed, or sites may have changed or ceased to exist since publication. While the author and publisher regret any inconvenience this may cause readers, no responsibility for any such changes can be accepted by either the author or the publisher.

CONTENTS

Video game revolution

What were the first words ever said in a video game?

What game lets you play as a giant hand?

How can playing video games give your doctor an edge?

Keep reading to learn the answers to these questions and more. Video games have come a long way in a short time. Just 50 years ago, today's technology was only a dream. Electronics and computer experts have turned it into reality.

Today's video games combine art, music, film-making and storytelling. Powerful software programs allow you to enter worlds beyond the imagination. In addition to gaming, this tech is being used to train workers for the future.

There is no telling where the video game revolution will lead. But it's fun to know where it all started.

CHAPTER 1

GREAT MOMENTS IN GAMING TECH

Electronics whizzes started making simple video games in the 1950s. *Bertie the Brain* was one of the first. It could play noughts and crosses.

What goes great with video games? Pizza! Nolan Bushnell saw the future and a fortune on a video game screen. He and partner Ted Dabney **founded** Atari. Atari was one of the first electronic game makers. But Bushnell didn't stop there. He later launched Chuck E Cheese's **arcades** in the United States. These electronic funhouses combine pizza and video games!

found set up or start something
arcade business with video games that you pay to use

0:2

Allan Alcorn designed Atari's first hit game. He programmed *Pong*. It was a simple electronic table tennis match that made a beeping noise. It was also the first popular video game to include sound effects.

In 1972–73, *Pong* was released in arcades. People loved it and its simple sound effects. A home version soon followed and sold like crazy.

"Strike! Ball! Out!" Those were the first words a video game ever uttered. They called the action in Intellivision's *Major League Baseball*. The game was released in 1979. High-tech **sound cards** didn't become part of game systems until 1989. Then video games really started making noise.

sound card computer hardware that allows software programs to produce sounds

CENTIPEDE™
COMPUTER
GAME

USE WITH JOYSTICK CONTROLLERS

ATARI CXL4020

Early video game programmers weren't always men. Dona Bailey was one of the women pioneers in the video game revolution. She teamed up with Ed Logg to create and design the 1981 arcade game, *Centipede*. It was a hit! She became a college lecturer for game design, teaching future designers.

Today's game consoles have lots of computing power. NASA's first space shuttle launched in 1981. Its flight computer had less than 1 per cent of the computing power of 2005's Xbox 360 game console. The 2017 Xbox One X has 24 times the computing power of the Xbox 360. More computing power means better computer **graphics** and faster play.

graphic visual image such as an illustration, photograph or work of art

Old video game graphics seem blocky compared to current graphics. More powerful computers made better graphics possible. Designers use polygons to build characters and scenes. The more polygons they can use, the clearer the image is. The first *Crash Bandicoot* game had about 512 polygons in 1996. Recent characters such as Nathan Drake in *Uncharted 4: A Thief's End* (2016) have about 90,000 polygons.

CHAPTER 2

GAME CHANGERS

Video games have gone from simple fun to high-powered action and strategy. Take a look at some wild facts about classic games.

The Japanese game-making company Square was about to go out of business in 1987. They were sure their new game would be their last. That's why they called it *Final Fantasy*. They should have called it *First and Forever Fantasy*. More than 30 years later, the series is still going strong. There are more than 15 *Final Fantasy* titles. The game has also inspired films and TV series.

Madden NFL is the best-selling sport video game ever. Nothing else comes close. It is named after John Madden, famous American football coach. The game updates its players every year. The game is so life-like that NFL quarterbacks Drew Brees and Teddy Bridgewater play it. They use the video game to work on their team's playbook.

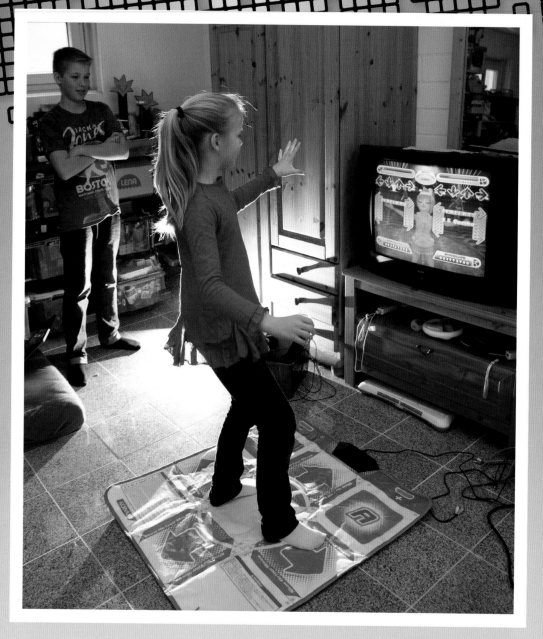

Video games can inspire new words such as "exergaming". *Dance, Dance Revolution* was one of the games associated with that term because of the workout it gives players. Some schools even feature *DDR* in PE classes. In "difficult mode", players can burn almost 25 calories per three-minute song.

Guitar Hero: Aerosmith was a game released in 2008. It sold more than 3 million copies by 2010. Sales of the rock band's music jumped 40 per cent afterwards. The game helped to **reboot** Aerosmith's fame.

> **reboot** start something again

People of all ages enjoy playing video games, but some are considered unsuitable for younger gamers. Just like films, video games are given age certificates. The British Board of Film Classification (BBFC) started rating video games in the UK in 1986. Since 2012, however, video games have been rated by the Video Standards Council (VSC) as either PEGI 12, 16 or 18, meaning it is illegal for people under that age to buy the game. *Mortal Kombat* is one example of a game that has an 18 certificate due to the strong violence it contains.

In 2006, Wii popularized a gaming system that allowed players to actually swing, throw and punch using motion-sensing technology. The first five games featured on *Wii Sports* were tennis, baseball, bowling, boxing and golf. Today, there are more than 1,200 titles playable on Wii. They range from *Alice in Wonderland* to *All-Star Karate*. Wii consoles rank among the best-sellers of all time.

Angry Birds features feathered friends battling green pigs. It has been the top-selling **app** at the online App Store for years. *Angry Birds Space* and *Angry Birds Seasons* have also been in the top 10. The game has inspired a film and several TV series.

"Electronic sports", or eSports, is gaining a big following. It has more than 300 million fans worldwide who watch as well as play. For professional gamers, *Defense of the Ancients 2* (*Dota2*) has been a favourite. The *Dota2* champ Saahil "Universe" Arora of the United States earned his first $1 million at the age of 25.

In Japan, *Dragon Quest* remains a classic role-playing game. The first game, *Dragon Warrior*, was released in 1986. Nintendo, the company that makes it, now only releases new versions on public holidays and weekends. Otherwise too many people take time off from work and school to play.

Online video gaming connects players around the world. *PlayerUnknown's Battlegrounds* regularly tops 1 million gamers at any one time, according to the SteamCharts website. Its peak was just over 3 million players in December 2017. That record probably won't last long.

app program that is downloaded to computers and mobile devices; app is short for application

CHAPTER 3

COOL CHARACTER FACTOIDS

One of the best parts of playing video games is that you can become your favourite character. But have you ever wondered how these characters came to be?

Sega designers wanted a fierce but loveable character for a new game. It came down to an armoured armadillo or a spiky hedgehog. *Sonic the Hedgehog* won that battle. He has been winning ever since. Naoto Ohshima designed *Sonic the Hedgehog*. How did he come up with the design? He says he put Felix the Cat's head on Mickey Mouse's body.

Designers wanted to create a new game featuring the cartoon character Popeye the Sailor. His opponent would be his muscle-bound rival Bluto. But Nintendo could not get permission to use these classic characters. Who did they create instead? They came up with *Donkey Kong*. The big ape faced off against a plumber with a floppy red hat and big moustache. You may have heard of him and his brother, Luigi. Today, Mario is the most recognizable character in video game history.

Bonus trivia:
When Mario's character was being developed, his original name was "Jumpman". And he wasn't a plumber. He was a carpenter.

Super Mario Galaxy includes a surprise **unlockable character**. Mario is the hero, as usual. He must rescue his taller, greener brother, Luigi. But if players accomplish certain goals they unlock Luigi. They can then play as a super-powered version of him. All it takes is collecting 120 stars and defeating Bowser in combat.

unlockable character hidden character a player must win the right to play

Lara Croft is one of the most popular video game heroes in history. At least 10 versions of the game have been made. In 2001 *Lara Croft: Tomb Raider* became the top-selling film based on a video game character. In 2018 a new version of the film was released.

The Temple of Ta Prohm, made famous by *Tomb Raider*

Sackboy is the good guy of *LittleBigPlanet*. This quirky game allows players to create and share new game levels. Sackboy zips around collecting bubbles and dressing up in the things he finds. He also proves there's more to being a hero than knocking out opponents. At the end, he faces his "boss fight" – a final big battle. His foe is The Collector. However, The Collector just turns out to be a lonely person. Sackboy wins the game by offering friendship.

Master Chief is the super-soldier in the *Halo* series. Game maker sources describe his character as standing about 2 metres (7 feet) tall. In his powered armour, he weighs 450 kilograms (1,000 pounds).

Actor Mark Hamill is most famous for playing Luke Skywalker in the *Star Wars* films. But for the game *Batman: Arkham City*, he went to the dark side. He voiced Batman's arch enemy, the Joker. Hamill perfected Joker's well-known crazy laugh.

Tony Hawk's *Pro Skater* collection features a few of the weirdest guest characters in gaming. Players can skate as Shrek, Benjamin Franklin and Spiderman. They can also choose to be a giant hand and other weird objects.

CHAPTER 4

FROM VIRTUAL TO REALITY

Today, video games are much more than fun and games. They have become part of popular culture and everyday life.

Video games are fun for the whole family. Almost six out of ten parents play video games with their kids, according to the Entertainment Software Association. About 60 per cent of players play with friends.

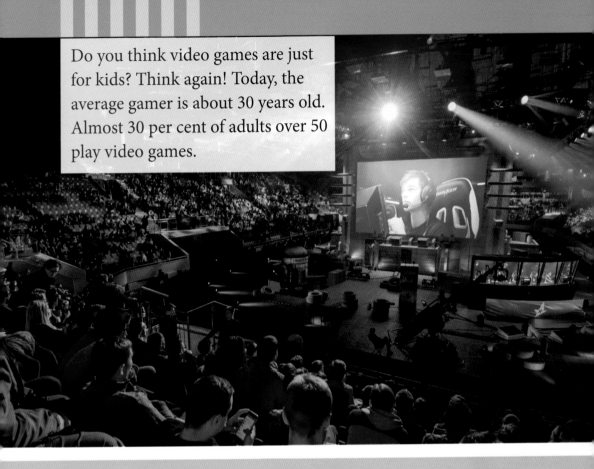

Do you think video games are just for kids? Think again! Today, the average gamer is about 30 years old. Almost 30 per cent of adults over 50 play video games.

Worldwide, there are more than 2 billion gamers. They have turned video games into a huge industry that earns almost $100 billion a year. That total is more than the music and film industries combined.

The military uses video game technology to train its soldiers and sailors. Even medics learn certain skills using **simulations**. Battle simulations allow them to train to handle dangerous situations. In a game, they do not have to risk their lives or blow up anything real.

Video games can help surgeons improve their skills at work. Laparoscopic surgery puts a camera and surgical tools inside a patient through a small cut. A 2003 study compared laparoscopic surgeons who regularly played video games to those who didn't. The gamers operated faster. They also made fewer mistakes than the other group.

More employers are using video game technology to train workers. Simulators allow pilots to practise flying aircraft. Software also teaches people to **navigate** huge ships, put out fires and operate giant cranes. The programs can simulate all kinds of weather. These simulators allow people to practise their duties without any real-life risk.

simulation computer model of something in real life

navigate steer a course

Gamescom is the biggest gaming convention in the world. In 2017 it drew more than 350,000 video game fans from 106 countries. More than 900 companies showed off their coolest games.

Video Games Live™ organizes international concerts. They perform music from popular video games. The orchestra plays songs from *Warcraft*, *Diablo*, *Myst* and several other fan favourites. As audience members listen, they see images from the games on large screens. This music series has been performed in cities around the world. Thanks to video streaming, 752,109 people saw the show performed in China in 2015. It set a Guinness World Record for this type of concert.

Some video games may help you relax and even get to sleep. Have you ever played *Tetris*? Studies show it can reduce stress and help people to sleep.

CHAPTER 5

THE NEXT FRONTIER

Video games and gaming grow and change very quickly. New technology and fresh ideas appear constantly.

"**Augmented reality** mobile experiences" take players outside. Games such as *Pokémon GO* and *Harry Potter: Wizards Unite*, allow gaming technology to interact with the real world.

augmented reality enhanced image or environment as viewed on a screen or other display

Game-design technology helped create the stadium for American football team the Dallas Cowboys. Architects used software to view the football field from every angle before it was built. This technology helps builders see possibilities and problems before they start building.

Some game developers are inviting players to help add to their games. These games include software tools so players can develop their own levels and twists. Players can then share their work online.

Video gaming has become a popular spectator sport. The International 7 gaming tournament in 2017 drew more than 20 million viewers. The International Olympic Committee is even considering adding eSports to the Olympic Games.

From *Bertie the Brain* to *Final Fantasy* and beyond, video gaming continues to change. It has grown from simple entertainment to a creative wonderland. The technology knows no limits. It is a source of real-world inspiration as well as fantastic fun.

Glossary

app program that is downloaded to computers and mobile devices; app is short for application

arcade business with video games that you pay to use

augmented reality enhanced image or environment as viewed on a screen or other display

found set up or start something

graphic visual image such as an illustration, photograph or work of art

navigate steer a course

reboot start something again

simulation computer model of something in real life

sound card computer hardware that allows software programs to produce sounds

unlockable character hidden character a player must win the right to play

Find out more

Books

Awesome Video Game Competitions, Lori Polydoros (Raintree, 2017)

Coding Games in Python, DK (DK Publishing, 2018)

Computer Games Designer (The Coolest Jobs on the Planet),
Mark Featherstone (Raintree, 2014)

STEAM Jobs for Gamers, Sam Rhodes (Raintree, 2018)

Websites

www.bbc.co.uk/guides/zchc4wx
Learn more about how video games work.

www.dkfindout.com/uk/computer-coding
Find out more about computer coding.

Index